568
Sa

Sandell, Elizabeth J.
Archaeopteryx: the first
bird

DEMCO

ARCHAEOPTERYX

THE FIRST BIRD

by

Elizabeth J. Sandell

DINOSAUR DISCOVERY ERA

Bancroft-Sage Publishing
533 8th St. So., Box 664, Naples, FL 33939-0664 USA

LIBRARY OF CONGRESS CATALOGING IN PUBLICATION DATA

Sandell, Elizabeth J.
  Archaeopteryx: the first bird.

  (Dinosaur discovery era)
  SUMMARY: Describes how paleontologists discovered and
reconstructed fossil remains of the small feathered creature which
resembled both dinosaurs and birds.
  1. Archaeopteryx--Juvenile literature. (1. Archaeopteryx. 2.
Dinosaurs. 3. Paleontology.) I. Oelerich, Marjorie L. II. Hansen,
Harlan S. III. Vista III Design. IV. Title. V. Series.
QE872.A8S26   1989   567.9'7   88-39803
  ISBN 0-944280-13-7 (lib. bdg.)
  ISBN 0-944280-19-6 (pbk bdg.)

International Standard Book Number:	Library of Congress Catalog Card Number:
Library Binding 0-944280-13-7	88-39803
Paperback Binding 0-944280-19-6	

SPECIAL THANKS FOR THEIR HELP AND COOPERATION TO:
Mary R. Carman, Paleontology Collection Manager
Field Museum of Natural History
Chicago, IL

John H. Ostrom, Ph.D., Professor of Geology
Peabody Museum of Natural History
Yale University, New Haven, CT

ARCHAEOPTERYX

THE FIRST BIRD

AUTHOR
Elizabeth J. Sandell

dedicated to Ben, Sam, and Molly Lien

EDITED BY
Marjorie L. Oelerich, Ph.D.
Professor of Early Childhood and Elementary Education
Mankato State University
Mankato, MN

Harlan S. Hansen, Ph.D.
Professor of Early Childhood and Elementary Education
University of Minnesota
Minneapolis, MN

ILLUSTRATED BY
Vista III Design

BANCROFT-SAGE PUBLISHING
533 8th St. So., Box 664, Naples, FL 33939-0664 USA

INTRODUCTION: DISCOVERING ARCHAEOPTERYX

"We have been learning a great deal about what might have happened when dinosaurs lived and died," Mr. Finley, the teacher, told the class.

"However, there is information we don't know about some other animals which were alive a long time ago. Let's play the game, Dinosaur Era Trivia, to review what we know and to learn some more," Mr. Finley suggested.

So, the students worked together in small groups to answer the questions in the game. Ryan became the leader of his team.

As he read a question from the game, his group would look in Dinosaur Discovery Era books to find any answers they did not already know.

"This is the first question," announced Ryan. "'What is a dinosaur?'"

"Dinosaur means terrible lizard," Rosa answered. "It is from two Greek words. **Deinos** means terrible, and **sauros** means lizard. However, now we know that dinosaurs were not lizards."

"That's right. Here is question number two. 'What scientists study dinosaurs?'" Ryan read from the game card.

The answer to that was found in one Dinosaur Discovery Era book.

"'Paleontologists study dinosaurs,'" read Rosa.

Ryan read the next question. "'What do paleontologists collect and study to find information about dinosaurs?'"

"Fossils!" Mychal quickly answered. "Those are stone-like remains of plants and animals from thousands of years ago."

"'What covered the bodies of dinosaurs?'" was the next question which Ryan read.

"I guess it was some kind of skin," Mychal suggested.

"'Scientists are studying what might have covered the bodies of dinosaurs,'" Ryan read from the Dinosaur Discovery Era book. "'They have found fossils of animals with feathers which lived about the time of dinosaurs. These animals are called *Archaeopteryx*. Some paleontologists think *Archaeopteryx* was a dinosaur. Others believe it was a bird.'"

"Feathers!" Mychal exclaimed. "I've never heard of a dinosaur with feathers! How could that be possible? Let's look for more information about *Archaeopteryx*."

The game of Dinosaur Era Trivia came to a sudden stop. The students wanted to know about the feathered animal which some scientists thought was a dinosaur and others thought was a bird.

For the next few days, the class studied about *Archaeopteryx*. They read the Dinosaur Discovery Era books. They visited a museum to see an exhibit of *Archaeopteryx*. And a paleontologist came to class to tell about this feathered animal. The paleontologist told how *Archaeopteryx* might have looked, how it probably lived, and how it might have died.

CHAPTER 1: ARCHAEOPTERYX HAD FEATHERS

When fossils of *Archaeopteryx* (ar ke op´ ter iks) were found, paleontologists were surprised to see the impression of feathers along the arms and tail. This made the scientists wonder whether this animal was a bird instead of a dinosaur.

Over one hundred years ago, Thomas Henry Huxley suggested that there was a similarity between dinosaurs and birds.

COMPARING ARCHAEOPTERYX TO DINOSAURS

There is information which shows that *Archaeopteryx* was like some dinosaurs.

In 1973, Dr. John Ostrom told ways in which *Archaeopteryx* was similar to a group of dinosaurs called *coelurosaurs* (so luhr´ uh sorz´). Here is Dr. Ostrom's list:

- The size of *Archaeopteryx* and some *coelurosaurs* was nearly the same.
- They both had long, bony tails.
- Their hips were alike.
- Their hind legs and feet were alike.

- They had two long hind legs.
- They had one toe that faced backward on each hind leg.
- They walked on these two hind legs.
- Their front legs were short and were like arms.
- Their arms were alike.
- They had claws on their front arms.
- They had long necks.
- They had pointed teeth.

However, there is one way in which *Archaeopteryx* was different from *coelurosaurs*.

- *Archaeopteryx* had feathers.

COMPARING ARCHAEOPTERYX TO BIRDS

Some scientists believe *Archaeopteryx* may have been the first bird. Of all the fossils which have been found, *Archaeopteryx* is the earliest animal which is known to have had feathers. Also, of all the animals alive today, birds are the only ones with feathers. Therefore, scientists compare fossils of *Archaeopteryx* with today's birds.

Dr. Ostrom reported several ways in which *Archaeopteryx* was very much like birds today. Here are some of these features:

- Both *Archaeopteryx* and birds had feathers.
- The size of *Archaeopteryx* and some birds was nearly the same.

- They both had wishbones made of collarbones that were joined.
- They had two hind legs.
- The hind legs and feet were slim.
- They had one toe that faced backwards on each hind leg.
- They walked on these two hind legs.
- They had long, slender necks.
- They had large eyes for the size of their head.
- They had large brains for their body size.
- They had long, narrow beaks.
- They ate insects.
- *Archaeopteryx* probably laid eggs in nests, like birds do. However, fossils of these nests and eggs have not been found.

There were some ways, too, that *Archaeopteryx* was different from birds.

- *Archaeopteryx* had narrow jaws with short, sharp teeth; birds have no teeth.
- *Archaeopteryx* had a long, bony tail which was covered with feathers. Many birds have a tail of feathers but with almost no bone. Some birds do have a bony tail, but it is not very long.
- *Archaeopteryx* had three separate, clawed fingers on its wing-like arms. Adult birds do not have clawed fingers.

13

FEATHERS AND WINGS

However, the most surprising parts of *Archaeopteryx* were the feathers and the wings.

Feathers covered the long, bony tail, which made this animal about 1 to 2 feet (30 to 60 cm) long. This is about the size of some birds, such as pigeons or crows, which are alive today.

Paleontologists believe that the feathers which covered this tail might have helped *Archaeopteryx* in several ways.

- The feathers might have helped to keep the body warm.
- The feathers could have provided balance while this animal was running.
- The feathers might have helped the animal to jump farther.
- The feathers may have helped the animal to change direction faster.

Feathers covered the two front arms, also. Scientists call these arms instead of legs, because the animal did not use them for walking or running.

Because these feathered arms looked something like wings, this animal was given the name *Archaeopteryx*, which means "ancient wing."

USE OF THE WING-LIKE ARMS

Scientists are not sure how *Archaeopteryx* used these wing-like front arms. Some scientists have wondered whether this animal could actually fly at all.

From examining fossil skeletons, scientists believe that if *Archaeopteryx* could have flown, it would not have been as strong a flyer as most birds are today. In fact, some scientists suggest that this animal was a poor flyer. Fossils show the chest bones probably were not able to hold muscles strong enough to allow this animal to fly well.

In an attempt to fly, *Archaeopteryx* might have used its front arms to push itself into the air. It might have taken off from the ground, then fluttered weakly. The wind may have helped to lift it so it could fly a short distance.

Perhaps *Archaeopteryx* may have used its wings to glide into the air from the trees. One edge of the animal's feathers was longer than the other edge. This is the kind of feather that is necessary for gliding.

Some scientists believe that *Archaeopteryx* may have lived most of its life in trees. It might have climbed into trees by using its strong hind legs and clawed fingers on its arms. Or it might have used its wings to flutter onto low branches.

If *Archaeopteryx* could get into trees, it might have been safe from enemies. Meat-eating animals, such as *Ornitholestes* (or nith´ o les´ teez) and *Coelurus* (so luhr´ us), were quick at catching small animals such as *Archaeopteryx* for food.

Other paleontologists do not believe that *Archaeopteryx* could have lived in trees. These scientists believe that the first toe on its foot was too short and too high to be helpful for sitting in trees.

The feathered arms may have helped *Archaeopteryx* makelittle jumps so it could catch flying insects. It also might have reached into the air with these wing-like arms to grab dragonflies and butterflies for food.

Some fossils of fish and other water animals have been found in the same rocks that preserve *Archaeopteryx*. This suggests that it may have been able to glide close to the water to catch fish swimming near the top.

CHAPTER 2:
THE WORLD OF ARCHAEOPTERYX

Archaeopteryx lived thousands of years ago. The weather may have been very mild. The summers were warm and wet, and there were no cold winters.

There were forests of palm trees, cycads, giant ferns, williamsonias, and other leafy plants. There were no flowering plants.

There were butterflies, dragonflies, and other insects like we have today.

JURASSIC

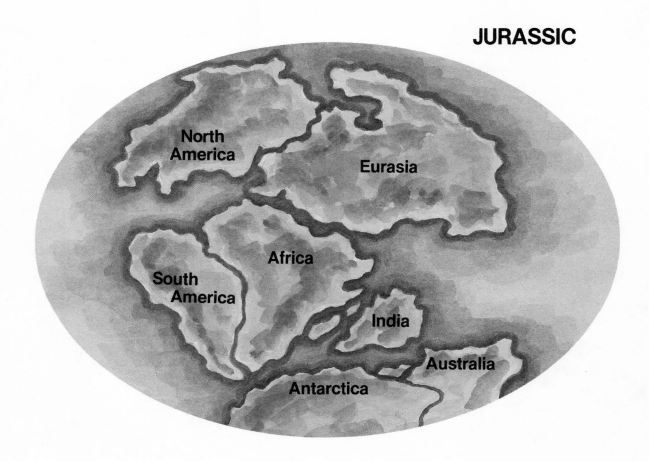

Over many years, earthquakes and volcanoes caused the land to change as it moved up and down. Some land rose up and became mountains. Other land became the bottom of rivers. Rocks where fossils were buried were pushed to the top of the earth. That is where scientists have been able to find fossils in recent years.

When *Archaeopteryx* lived, the land may have been joined like the map above. There were connections between the land masses, so that animals had large areas to roam.

CHAPTER 3:
FINDING FOSSILS OF
ARCHAEOPTERYX

Scientists do not know whether *Archaeopteryx* traveled throughout all of these land areas. It is possible that this animal stayed mostly in one region. In fact, all six fossil skeletons of *Archaeopteryx* have been found in Europe. None have been discovered elsewhere.

Fossil bones of *Archaeopteryx* were found in layers of rock. Sometimes, when an *Archaeopteryx* died, its body might have been covered with mud. This muddy water, which contained minerals, would get into every part of the bones. Then, the minerals would turn the bones into hard rock, which we call fossils.

The earliest fossils of this animal had been found in 1855, in the region of Solnhofen, West Germany (Europe). At that time, scientists did not know that some of these fossils were from *Archaeopteryx*. It was not until 1970 that many of these fossils were identified as leg and wing bones of an *Archaeopteryx*. Dr. John Ostrom was studying a collection of other fossils at Teyler Stichting Museum in Haarlem, The Netherlands (Europe). As he carefully examined these fossils, he recognized that one of them preserved parts of an *Archaeopteryx*.

In 1861, Dr. Karl Haberlein also found a fossil skeleton of *Archaeopteryx* in a quarry near Solnhofen, West Germany (Europe). This skeleton did not have a skull. However, the skull was later found.

A few years later, scientists learned that *Archaeopteryx* had teeth. In 1877, Dr. Ernst Haberlein, whose father was Dr. Karl Haberlein, found a skeleton that included a skull. There were fossil teeth in this skull.

An *Archaeopteryx* skeleton, found in 1950, was thought to be a *Compsognathus* (komp´ so nay´ thus). However, in 1974, Dr. Peter Wellnhofer carefully studied this fossil. He described it as an *Archaeopteryx*, not a *Compsognathus*.

Another fossil skeleton of *Archaeopteryx* without a head was found in 1956. This skeleton is called the Maxberg *Archaeopteryx*, because it was shown in a museum for many years in Maxberg, West Germany (Europe). The owner has now decided to keep it in his possession. Therefore, it is no longer on display.

The largest fossil of *Archaeopteryx* was announced in June, 1988, by Dr. Peter Wellnhofer. It had been found a number of years earlier by F. Muller, who collected fossils. This discovery was in a quarry near Eichstatt, West Germany (Europe).

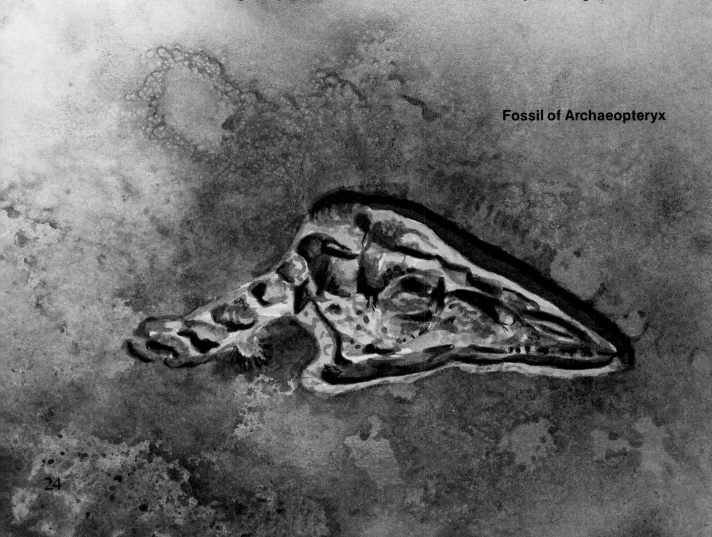

Fossil of Archaeopteryx

Drawing of Archaeopteryx skeleton

CHAPTER 4:
WHY ARCHAEOPTERYX DISAPPEARED

With so few known fossils of *Archaeopteryx*, scientists have many questions about the death of this animal. There are many different ideas about these questions. Somehow the air on earth changed. This might have been caused by several lumps of rock about six miles (10 km) across that crashed into earth from space. A cloud of dust from the crash might have blocked out the sunlight and caused a change in the weather. Perhaps *Archaeopteryx* was unable to survive this change.

Other reasons for the death of these animals might have been disease, a flood, or some enemies.

No one really knows for sure why they died. It may have taken thousands of years, but all the animals known as *Archaeopteryx* are gone.

CONCLUSION:
STILL MORE TO LEARN

"We've learned a lot about *Archaeopteryx*," said Mr. Finley.

"Now, Ryan, for the game of Dinosaur Era Trivia, name some facts we learned about *Archaeopteryx*," continued Mr. Finley. "Also, name some things which we do not know about this animal."

Ryan and his team hurried to think of what they had learned about *Archaeopteryx*.

1. *Archaeopteryx* might have been the first bird.
2. Its front legs were short and were something like arms.
3. These front arms might have looked like wings.
4. It had feathers on these front arms.
5. *Archaeopteryx* had feathers on its tail.
6. Only six skeletons of *Archaeopteryx* have been found to date.
7. No *Archaeopteryx* animals are alive today.

Ryan's team also thought of information which is not known about *Archaeopteryx*.

1. We do not know for sure whether *Archaeopteryx* was a dinosaur or a bird.
2. We do not know if *Archaeopteryx* could really fly with its wings.
3. We do not know why all the *Archaeopteryx* animals are gone.

"That was exciting!" commented Mychal. "Let's study more about *Archaeopteryx*, dinosaurs, and birds, so we can play this game again!"

MUSEUMS

We can see fossils of *Archaeopteryx* only in museums. Of the six known skeletons, five of them are in exhibits.

Here are the places where we can see displays of *Archaeopteryx* today.

Bergermeister Museum, Solnhofen, West Germany (Europe).

British Museum of Natural History, London, England (Europe).

Humboldt Museum of Natural History, East Berlin, East Germany (Europe).

Juramuseum, Eichstatt, West Germany (Europe).

Teyler Stichting, Haarlem, The Netherlands (Europe).

GLOSSARY

ARCHAEOPTERYX (ar ke op´ ter iks) means "ancient wing." The Greek word **archaios** means "ancient," and the word **pteryx** means "wing." This was the first feathered animal. Some scientists think that it was the first bird.

COELURUS (so luhr´ us) means "hollow bones." The Greek word **koilos** means "hollow" and refers to the hollow bones in its tail. This was a small meat-eater which walked on its two back feet. It may have been 5 feet (1.5 m) long and 3 feet (91 cm) tall.

COELUROSAUR (so luhr´ uh sor´) is the name of a group of dinosaurs. The Greek word **koilos,** which means "hollow," was combined with the word **sauros,** which means "lizard." These dinosaurs had hollow bones. Now we know that coelurosaurs were not lizards.

COMPSOGNATHUS (komp´ so nay´ thus) means "elegant jaw," from the Greek words **kompos,** which means "elegant" or "pretty," and **gnathos,** which means "jaw." One of the smallest dinosaurs, it was only the size of a chicken. Compsognathus had hollow bones, a small and pointed head, sharp teeth, and a flexible neck. It moved very quickly on its two hind feet. Its hind legs were long, like the legs of birds. Each short, front leg had two claws. It probably used the claws to catch insects and small reptiles. Fossils of Compsognathus were found in Germany and in France (Europe).

DINOSAUR (di´ nuh sor´) means "terrible lizard." The Greek word **deinos** means "terrible," and the word **sauros** means "lizard." Dinosaurs, however, were not lizards.

FOSSILS (fos´ uhlz) are the remains of plants and animals that lived many years ago. The Latin word **fossilis** means "something dug up."

LIZARD (liz´ uhrd) is a kind of reptile. Most lizards are small with slender, scaly bodies; long tails; and four legs. Dinosaurs were not lizards.

MINERALS (min´ uhr ulz) are parts of water, rocks, and land that are not plants or animals.

MUSEUM (myoo ze´ uhm) is a place for keeping and exhibiting works of nature and art, scientific objects, and other items.

ORNITHOLESTES (or nith´ o les´ teez) means "bird robber." The Greek word **ornithos** means "bird," and the word **lestes** means "robber," because scientists imagined that it caught birds to eat. It was a coelurosaur which lived in North America. Skeletons have been found in Wyoming (USA).

PALEONTOLOGIST (pa´ le on tol´ uh jist) is a person who studies fossils to learn about plants and animals from thousands of years ago. The Greek word **palaios** means "ancient," **onta** means "living things," and **logos** means "talking about."

QUARRY (kwor´ e) is a place from which stone is taken by cutting, digging, or blasting.

SCIENTIST (si´ uhn tist) is a person who studies objects or events.

SKELETON (skel´ uh tuhn) is the framework of bones of a body.

THOUSAND (thou´ zuhnd) is ten times one hundred. It is shown as 1,000.

TIME LINE

PERIOD	CHARACTERISTIC ANIMAL LIFE
CRETACEOUS 65 MILLION YEARS TO 135 MILLION YEARS AGO	Triceratops, Pteranodon, Maiasaura, Tyrannosaurus rex, Plesiosaurus, Ankylosaurus
JURASSIC 136 MILLION YEARS TO 192 MILLION YEARS AGO	Apatosaurus, Allosaurus, Stegosaurus, Archaeopteryx, Compsognathus, Seismosaurus
TRIASSIC 193 MILLION YEARS TO 224 MILLION YEARS AGO	Mastodonsaurus, Rutiodon, Protosuchus, Plateosaurus
PERMIAN 225 MILLION YEARS TO 279 MILLION YEARS AGO	Eryops, Seymouria, Dimetrodon, Titanophoneus
CARBONIFEROUS 280 MILLION YEARS TO 345 MILLION YEARS AGO	Urocordylus, Hylonomus, Branchiosaurus

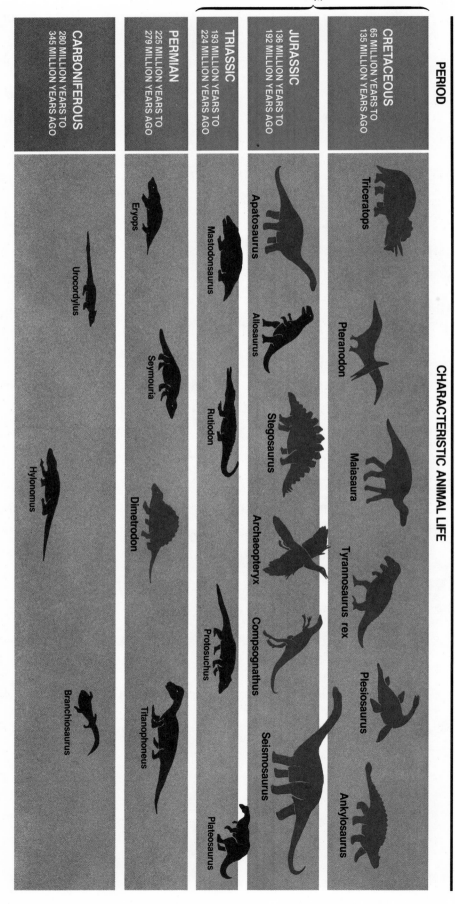